THE
THREE RIVERS

Walter C. Kidney

D1597158

Published by
Pittsburgh History & Landmarks Foundation
One Landmarks Square, Pittsburgh, PA 15212

Copyright © 1982
Pittsburgh History & Landmarks Foundation

Library of Congress Catalogue Card No. 82-81782
ISBN 0-916670-07-4

Printed in U.S.A.
First Edition

Partial funding for the writing of this book was provided by Dravo Corporation, Ohio Barge Line, Inc.,
Calgon Corporation, W. W. Patterson Company,
and the River Terminal Operators' Association.

CONTENTS

Centennial celebration of steamboat navigation on the Western Rivers; Pittsburgh, October 31, 1911.

WHAT A RIVER CAN BE

Depending on your viewpoint, a river can be a scene of natural beauty, a wealth-bringing highway, a half-noticed obstacle on a bridge crossing, a gift of God, or an unpredictable force that can damage property. The child, fascinated far away by so much water in one place, may sooner or later have a chance to approach the river and know it more intimately as something to wade in, fish in, or splash around. The excursionist, coming on board, gets an obscure pleasure from the very slight unsteadiness of the deck beneath his feet. The commuter, making the best time he can into town, may never really see the river, but the engineer who provided the bridge he crosses was profoundly aware of it in terms of dimensions, rates of flow, channels to keep free, and the geological structure beneath. The pilot, easing a floating mass 1,150 feet long and 105 feet wide along the river, imagines the channel he is to follow regardless of the width of its surface. The shipper, whose wish the pilot fulfills, imagines a line of a certain length along which a certain number of tons of a certain material will proceed during a certain period at a certain rate per ton/mile. Wet feet or dry figures: a river means many things to many people. □

THE MAKING OF WESTERN PENNSYLVANIA

Three hundred million years ago, Pennsylvania was crossed by two great rivers, running westward. The present location of Pittsburgh was delta land, being built up from the deposits of mud and sand that the southern river hustled along, then dropped as its water slowed down at the edge of a great inland sea. Eventually the mud, compacted under later deposits, became shale, while the sand became sandstone. Plants growing in the delta mud died, were buried, and turned under pressure into coal. Animals in the inland sea died too, and their skeletons became limestone.

The earth's crust was still forming from plate-like masses, and east-west pressures folded one such plate to form the Allegheny Mountains, which cut off the great rivers. Then erosion attacked the mountains and the mineral layers as new rivers and smaller streams found their way downhill. Pittsburgh's hills are actually what are left of the deposited minerals of millions of years ago after erosion by these newer rivers.

In the Ice Age, four glaciers invaded the present area of the United States. By this time the inland sea had retreated into the present Great Lakes area. Two of the glaciers affected Pennsylvania. The Illinois Glacier pushed aside the existing streams, and it also pushed a great apron of gravel and boulders before it into the hollows in the land. Eleven thousand years ago the last glacier, the Wisconsin, pushed down still more material. The glacier itself did not get near Pittsburgh, but the masses of boulders, gravel, and sand it moved before it did get there, and still form the bases of the Golden Triangle, the North Side, the South Side, and other neighborhoods on the river plains. □

Pennsylvania 300 million years ago.

THE THREE RIVERS

The Ohio

The Ohio River, the Belle Rivière of the seventeenth-century French, is 981 miles long. It begins at the Pittsburgh Point and discharges into the Mississippi at Cairo, Illinois, and in that distance it falls from 710 feet above sea level to about 275. It has not the drama of the Mississippi — the sheer size, the destructive whimsy — but navigators have found it a river to respect nonetheless, and yet worth the effort it has taken to tame it. Left to itself, it would flood badly — 204,000 square miles of land drain into it — or go frustratingly dry. Early navigators had to contend with its fluctuations, and with rapids, rocks, and snags as well. Their steadiest problem was the so-called Falls at Louisville, a set of descending rapids that divided the Lower from the Upper Ohio, which could be navigated safely only when the water was high.

Looking toward the Pittsburgh Point, where the Allegheny and Monongahela rivers join to form the Ohio. All three of our rivers take their names from Indian words. Ohio means "beautiful river" in Seneca. Allegheny may mean the same or *it may come from Allegwi-hanna, "stream of the Allegwi," who were a local tribe. Monongahela is from menaungehilla, "high, crumbling banks."*

The Allegheny

The Allegheny River, in the eighteenth century, was often considered part of the Ohio by the English, rightly enough since it contributes most of the Ohio's water at its origin: two billion gallons on a normal day versus the Monongahela's 755 million. Even so, its navigational history has been a checkered one, and today it is more for pleasure than use. The great navigational days for the Allegheny were during the reckless lumbering period from the mid-nineteenth century through the first quarter of this one, and especially during the frantic Oil Boom of the 1860s. Commercial navigation today goes about 60 miles up from the Point, and for the rest of its 325 miles the river runs through fairly unexploited, sometimes beautiful, country: hills, forests, wooded bog, and farmland; past Olean, New York, then back into Pennsylvania to its origin in Potter County near Coudersport. Its peaceful summer appearance today, under re-

straint of dams, gives no idea of the way it once could be in early spring, when snow and ice jams melted, and the Allegheny released a torrent so big and fast that its ice sometimes reached the Mississippi still frozen. Many an immigrant family, embarked on a flatboat from Olean, New York, or from the Johnstown Point at the head of the Conemaugh, was flushed down toward its new home on the chilly, perilous, rapid water of the Allegheny in early spring.

The Allegheny from Tidioute Overlook, far up the river at the edge of the Allegheny National Forest.

Oil Creek during the Oil Boom of the 1860s. Sometimes artificial dams were built, then smashed apart to give a fleet of flatboats a good start on their way to the Allegheny and the oil-refining center that Pittsburgh then was.

The Allegheny at Pittsburgh (below) and at Tidioute (opposite) seem like two different rivers: one spanned by many bridges in the heart of the city; the other winding through wooded forest.

The Monongahela

The Monongahela has always been a utilitarian river, ever since the first Europeans settled near it in the 1760s. It begins 127 miles upstream at Fairmont, West Virginia, at the confluence of the Tygart and the West Fork rivers, and is joined later by the Cheat and the Youghiogheny. Its future was decided by the early settlement of the region, the presence of coal near by, and the arrival of the National Road from Cumberland in 1817: industry, and particularly boat building and operation, were in its destiny. Old and dignified towns like Birmingham (now Pittsburgh's South Side), Brownsville, Monongahela, and Elizabeth have, when nothing more, a memory of prosperous times. Later towns, which thrived in a confused air of fire and smoke, have not the same quality of sedate assurance, reflected in old architecture, that these older places do. Regardless of a few good buildings, there is a sullen pettiness about the later industrial towns against the overriding trusswork of river bridges and the fantastic industrial constructions that rise above and behind them. The Monongahela Valley, in general, is engineer's, not architect's country. □

The historic neighborhood of Birmingham nestles on the slopes and flats of the South Side, along a bend of the Monongahela with the corporate towers of downtown Pittsburgh in view.

FRENCH VERSUS BRITISH

Early in the eighteenth century, two growing American empires were moving slowly on collision courses toward the Forks of the Ohio, the place we now call the Pittsburgh Point. The French were already established in the Montreal-Quebec area of Canada and in the Louisiana Territory, and had forts and settlements in the present states of Illinois, Indiana and Ohio. Their ambition was to secure a virtually all-water route between the two colonies: the St. Lawrence, Lakes Ontario and Erie, portage from the latter's south shore to French Creek, then down the Allegheny, Ohio, and Mississippi. The British, thus far held back by the Appalachian Mountains and by the Indians, had become ambitious for trade and land, and were getting aggressive. As the rivalry grew, the local Indians found themselves forced to take sides, and naturally looked for the best deals they could get, especially in trade. The indigenous Monongahela People had just disappeared (no one knows why), and Southwestern Pennsylvania was inhabited by Delawares, Shawnees, Ottawas, Mingoes, and Wyandots, to be wooed by the Europeans when possible and fought if necessary.

In 1753 the French built Forts Machault and LeBoeuf (the present locations of Franklin and Waterford, Pennsylvania) to defend French Creek. Learning of this, Governor Robert Dinwiddie of Virginia sent the 21-year-old George Washington to spy out the land and claim the territory formally for the British crown. At LeBoeuf, Washington was received politely but returned with a firm "No" to Virginia, after an adventurous winter journey that included his famous crossing of the Allegheny to present-day Lawrenceville. In 1754 a party of Virginians was foiled in their attempt to build Fort Prince George at the Point by the arrival of a French force that outnumbered them ten to one. The French promptly replaced Fort Prince George with their own Fort Duquesne, named after the energetic Governor of Canada, the Marquis du Quesne de Menneville. Later in 1754 the French

and Indian War — five years of heroism, stupidity, and brutality — began formally, or at least explicitly. The French, losing ground, abandoned and burned Fort Duquesne on November 24, 1758. Three days later the British victor, General John Forbes, proposed calling the new town anticipated for the site Pittsburgh, in honor of the British Prime Minister, William Pitt, Earl of Chatham. In 1759 the French gave up all land east of Detroit between Canada and the Louisiana Territory. Fort Pitt, the mightiest fortress yet built by the British in America, was completed in 1761: just as well, too, because in 1763 the new military post of 630 persons was under siege. □

"The Wine, as they dosed themselves pretty plentifully with it, soon banished the Restraint which at first appeared in their Conversation; and gave a Licence to their Tongues to reveal their Sentiments more freely.
"They told me, That it was their absolute Design to take Possession of the **Ohio,** *and by G——— they would do it."*
—Major George Washington on his visit to Fort Machault.

The twenty-one-year-old George Washington and his guide, Christopher Gist, crossed the Allegheny River just above the Point on December 30, 1753. When the raft jammed in the ice, Washington tried to free it; in doing so, he fell into the icy water and nearly drowned.

Marquis du Quesne de Menneville, Governor of Canada from 1752 to 1755, engineered the plan to create an all-water route guarded by French forts between Canada and Louisiana, thereby confining the British to the Eastern Seaboard.

Fort Duquesne (top), built in 1754, was situated directly at the Point. The British had a low opinion of it; it was liable to flooding, was too small for an effective garrison, was vulnerable to fire, and had only a few cannon. Fort Pitt (below) was much bigger — with its outworks, it was half the area of the modern Point State Park — and was planned and sited in a much more scientific way.

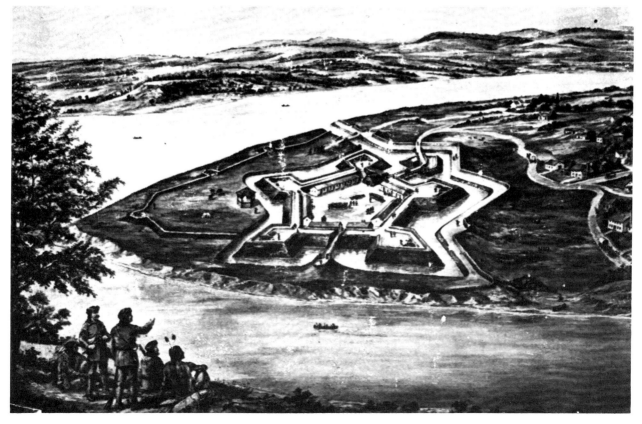

OPENING THE WEST

Relations with the Indians had continued to be uneasy. British land claims, exploitation by traders, and the weakening effects of rum and new European diseases kept them resentful, and in 1763 the Ottawa chief Pontiac led an alliance of tribes to strike back. It was too late, though, as the Indians eventually realized. In 1765 George Croghan, a veteran trader who had built up a western commercial empire, hunted down Pontiac in Indiana and talked him into accepting peace terms. Then he moved on to a round of councils with other Indian leaders, persuading them to open the Middle West and closer areas to trade and a vaguely paternalistic British presence.

Croghan's diplomacy did not completely end the Indian threat — that had to wait until 1794, when General Anthony Wayne won the Battle of Fallen Timbers (near Toledo, Ohio) — but it did encourage settlement, which soon became massive. In 1770 there were 5,000 settlers south of Pittsburgh, many of them from Virginia; five years later, there were 50,000. Immigrants began to move down the Ohio River too, as Congress established the Northwest Territory — the northern part of the Middle West — and passed an ordinance for its government in 1787. Louisville was founded as early as 1779, the important Ohio River town of Marietta in 1788, and Cincinnati (at first called Losantiville) in the same year. In 1803 we bought the Louisiana Territory — in other words, most of the present United States between the Mississippi and the Rocky Mountains — from Napoleon.

A gigantic area, in a few years, had become wide open to settlement and trade, and the Ohio River was *the* way to get to most of it. There was a fever on people, first Easterners discontent with conditions there, then foreigners, to go west. Some of these embarked at Olean, New York, far up the Allegheny, at the Johnstown Point on the Conemaugh, at Brownsville on the Monongahela, or at Wheeling down the Ohio; but many came into the Pittsburgh area to camp and to be exploited by boat builders, farmers, and merchants of all sorts while they waited for the river to rise in early spring. Sixteen thousand immigrants went through Pittsburgh between October 1786 and December 1788, and 13,000 went through in 1794 alone.

Naturally, Pittsburgh profited and grew. When Congress decided, in 1779, that Southwestern Pennsylvania *was* in Pennsylvania, and not in Virginia as the Virginians had been claiming, the Penns sold to the town some of their personally-owned "manor" land and commissioned George Woods and Thomas Vickroy to create a street plan. This, drawn in 1784, included all of the Golden Triangle. Pittsburgh's long-time rival Allegheny (now the North Side) was surveyed in 1788, lost its intended status as seat of Allegheny County to Pittsburgh in 1791, and was finally swallowed up by Pittsburgh in 1907, as many other towns already had been. In 1790 Pittsburgh had 376 inhabitants, in 1810 4,700, and in 1850 47,000. Cincinnati, for comparison, had 2,500 in 1810 and 115,000 in 1850; Louisville, 1,400 and 43,000 in these same years.

An Embarkation at Olean
"On Saturday night sat up late, heard some cracking of the ice, several of us observing that we should soon be on our way went to bed. Next morning at daylight found the river nearly clear, and at eight o'clock it was completely so. The place now presented a curious sight; the men conveying their goods on board the boats and rafts, the women scolding, and children crying, some clothed, and some half clothed, all in haste, filled with anxiety, as if a few minutes were lost the passage would be lost also. By ten o'clock the whole river for one mile appeared to be one solid body of boats and rafts. What, just before, appeared a considerable village, now remained but a few solitary huts with their occupants."
—Tilly Buttrick, 1815.

"It seems as if people were mad to git afloat on the Ohio."

– Israel Shreve, 1788, while leading New Jersey veterans westward.

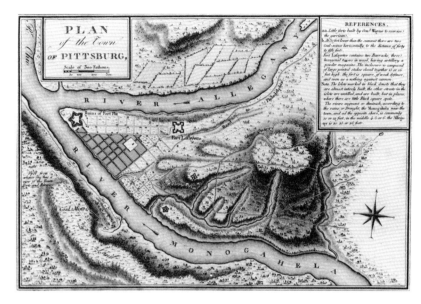

"Plan of the Town of Pittsburg" [sic] from the atlas of A Journey to North America, *by Victor Collot, published in 1826. Most of the Woods-Vickroy plan of 1784 is sketched in, though much of it remains to be built up. Fort Pitt is already in ruins, 65 years after construction. The new focus of the town is the "Diamond," the present Market Square, with the first Allegheny County Courthouse at its center since the 1790s though not shown here.*

This print, titled View of the City of Pittsburgh in 1817, *was made from a sketch by a Philadelphian, Mrs. Gibson, while on her wedding tour of the West. To the right, industrial smoke indicates the future of what still seems to be a village. The first Courthouse is the most prominent building. The flatboat, left foreground, seems to be going improbably upstream.*

13

In the long run, Pittsburgh grew as a manufacturing town rather than an embarkation point. In late summer the depth of the Ohio at Pittsburgh was measured in inches rather than feet, and the opening of the National Road from Cumberland and indirectly from Baltimore gave Brownsville and Wheeling a great advantage in the immigrant trades: Brownsville as the first port the road reached, Wheeling because it was further down the Ohio and thus offered a less frustrating flatboat trip in drought times than Pittsburgh. Later on, Pittsburgh's communications improved: the first Pennsylvania Turnpike, a first-class road to Lancaster and indirectly to Philadelphia, opened in 1820; a cross-state rail and canal system reached Pittsburgh in 1834 and other canals connected the Pittsburgh area with the Great Lakes; all-rail service with Philadelphia came in 1852 and with Chicago in 1858.

Yet Pittsburgh's destiny was an industrial one. In the years when communication with the East was bad, self-sufficiency was an obvious goal even had there been no masses of immigrants and downriver settlers clamoring for supplies. The first blast furnace west of the Alleghenies was probably the Alliance Iron Furnace of 1790, on Jacobs Creek off the Youghiogheny, owned by two men who were also partners in a distillery, a sawmill, a boatyard, and a saltworks. In 1793 the first furnace in the present city limits

Looking up the Ohio toward the Point and the already-celebrated Pittsburgh smoke in 1843: a painting of the J.M. Snowden saltworks next to Saw Mill Run by Russell Smith, an early recorder of the local scene.

was started, in Shadyside, by George Anshutz; this soon failed for want of ore, and Pittsburgh itself was not to have another blast furnace until 1859. The first Pittsburgh glass factory started in 1797, and window panes were being made in Allegheny in 1800. The Bakewell Glass House, once world-famous, began in 1807. Tin plating was noted in 1802, ironware manufacturing in 1803, a cotton mill in 1804, iron founding in 1805, a steam rolling mill in 1812, and engine-building in 1813. In 1790 the town was already smoky, though the coal back then must have been used mainly in domestic fires. □

"Pittsburgh Sketches — Among the Glassworkers"; Every Saturday, March 18, 1871.

The Jones & Laughlin Pittsburgh plant around 1960.

Before Steam on the Rivers

When people think of the Western Rivers — which is what the Mississippi and any navigable stream whose waters end there used to be called — they think of the paddle steamers. But thousands of craft moved on the rivers without the aid of engines until late in the nineteenth century. The pirogue, a dug-out canoe, was a pioneer craft, and so was the bateau, a broad, skiff-like rowboat. Among other things, ocean-going sailing vessels were once built on the Ohio, the Monongahela, and other streams around Pittsburgh, from the sloop *Western Experiment* of 1792 to the schooner *Locust Tree*, built at Sharon in 1851. Most of these were small craft, put in the coastal trade after arrival at New Orleans, but the Pittsburgh brig *Dean* crossed to Liverpool in 1803 with cotton. There is a hardy perennial story of an American captain arrested for customs fraud at Marseilles (or was it somewhere in Italy?) on the grounds that there was no such port as Pittsburgh.

The flatboat is the most famous of all the early boats, used by immigrant parties and by traders up to 1870. It was simply a box that drifted downriver, steered by long oars

called sweeps. It was usually launched in early spring, when the river, fed by rain and melting ice, flowed high and fast. At its destination it was sold for lumber. Variants were called arks, broadhorns, Kentucky boats, and New Orleans boats. There were also guiphers, flatboats used during the Oil Boom of the 1860s to take barreled oil from Oil Creek to the refineries at Pittsburgh. The bulkboat was another Oil Creek specialty, probably the world's first oil tanker. It was a reusable barge, sent to St. Louis and New Orleans in tows from 1865 on.

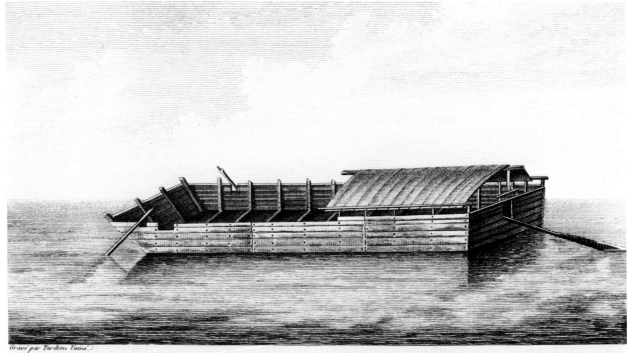

Sketch of a Flat bottom Boat, such as are used to descend the Ohio and the Mississippi.

Coalboats measured 175 feet by 26 feet like a modern Monongahela River barge. Usually the bottom of the coalboat was built up the Allegheny or on French Creek, laden with local produce, and sent down the river to be completed at a "siding yard" such as that shown here; afterwards, it went up the Monongahela for regular service.

"The last of the flatboats," drifting down the Mississippi shortly before 1900 with its crew resting at the sweeps.

The raft was quite common on the Allegheny during the reckless lumbering period of the mid- and late-nineteenth century, when awesome amounts of logs and cut timber floated down to Pittsburgh. One hundred raft arrivals there were recorded in a 24-hour period in 1851; 1,100 rafts came from one Allegheny tributary in 1859; and in the spring of 1857, two-thirds of a billion board feet of timber came to Pittsburgh.

Shantyboats — houseboats of a decidedly humble character — could be found on the rivers too. This photo, dating from some time around 1900, was probably taken near Sistersville, West Virginia.

The Legendary Mike Fink

Mike Fink, here imaginatively portrayed by William Gropper, was a larger-than-life Pittsburgher who made a spectacular macho reputation as he helped manhandle keelboats up and down the rivers. In the early 1790s he was an Indian fighter with General Anthony Wayne; during the War of 1812, the restless hero left the rivers and eventually died a violent death far west, along the Yellowstone. In between, he gave life to a legend. One reason was his mastery of rhetoric:

"I'm a Salt River roarer! I'm a ring-tailed squealer! I'm a reg'lar screamer from the ol' Massassip'! WHOOP! I'm the very infant that refused his milk before its eyes were open, and called out for a bottle of old Rye! I love the women an' I'm chockful o' fight! I'm half wild horse and half cock-eyed alligator and the rest o' me is crooked snags an' red-hot snappin' turkle. I can hit like fourth-proof lightnin' an' every lick I make in the woods lets in an acre o' sunshine. I can out-run, out-jump, out-shoot, out-brag, out-drink, an' out-fight, rough-an'-tumble, no holts barred, ary man on both sides the river from Pittsburgh to New Orleans an' back ag'in to St. Louiee. Come on, you flatters, you bargers, you milk-white mechanics, an' see how tough I am to chaw! I ain't had a fight for two days an' I'm spilein' for exercise. Cock-a-doodle-doo!"

MIKE FINK   GROPPER

The graceful keelboat (pictured here with a flatboat) was a relatively sophisticated product of the 1780s, used upstream as well as down and sharp-ended with ribs and a keel. It drifted or was rowed, poled, or sailed downstream; upstream it was moved by poling, cordelling (hauling, Volga-boatman-style, from shore), warping (pulling on ropes tied to trees), or bushwhacking (grabbing bushes and pulling). The legendary Mike Fink was a keelboatman.

THE WESTERN RIVER BOAT

Among all these industries, the building, equipping, and operation of boats was eminent. Pittsburgh was not alone in this; in the steamboat period, the whole Upper Ohio and Lower Monongahela area was to be active in boatbuilding, with Pittsburgh, Cincinnati, and Louisville producing four-fifths of all the steamboat tonnage on the Western Rivers; only St. Louis was a serious rival, and then only after 1840. Beginning in 1811, when Robert Fulton's *New Orleans* was built at about the place where the Light Rail route enters the Triangle at the foot of Duquesne University, and up to 1880, Pittsburgh alone built almost *one third* of all Western River tonnage: 1,760 steamboats in all.

A keelboat round trip to Louisville took two months; an upriver trip from St. Louis took three. This was very slow, expensive going, dependent wholly on the muscle power of Mike Fink and his companions. How a Pittsburgh cotton mill in 1804, even though it must have been a small, almost-handicraft operation, got a sufficient affordable supply from the South is a mystery of economics. Something had to be done. A foretaste of the solution had come in 1761 at Fort Pitt, when William Ramsey experimented with a pedal-operated sidewheeler. Had a workable engine been available, it might have hastened still further the development of the West. But 1761 knew only the atmospheric engine, in which the air worked against an induced vacuum, and even this massive and fuelwasting engine, incapable of rotary motion, was represented in the Western Hemisphere by only one example. In 1803 James McKeever almost got a steamboat on the water at New Orleans, using a modern steam engine by the Philadelphia industrialist Oliver Evans, but river conditions so discouraged him that he handed the engine over to a sawmill.

James Rees & Sons Company was a celebrated Pittsburgh builder of steamboat engines and — very unusually — of metal steamers. The company lasted from 1845 to 1932. Here, two steamers for Latin America are under construction.

In 1807, Robert Fulton's *North River Boat of Clermont,* a sidewheeler, opened commercial steam navigation on the Hudson, and Fulton and his partners soon turned their attention to the Western Rivers, naturals for power craft. In 1811 the *New Orleans,* the first steamer for this service, was launched at Pittsburgh, made its way down to its name city, found the current too strong for its feeble power to attempt a return, and stayed on the Lower Mississippi. It was 1815 before the *Enterprise,* built by Brownsville citizens Daniel French and Henry Miller Shreve, became the first steamer to make a round trip. Shreve, who has been credited with many of the improvements to Western River steam navigation, was also one of those who attempted and eventually managed to break the monopoly there that Fulton had tried to establish.

One major problem — in fact, *the* major problem — that Fulton and other early builders faced was that steam navigation on the Western Rivers required a new kind of boat. On the one hand, wave action that might rack the hull at sea was almost negligible on the rivers. On the other, the rivers themselves had wild fluctuations in depth; the Ohio at Wheeling varied, *on the average,* between 18 inches and 33 feet in depth. The situation called for a boat that was light in weight and shallow in draft, even at the price of flimsiness, and the builders groped toward a solution. The early boats were built according to conventional seagoing practice as modified by what little was understood about steam engineering. They had deep holds, in which the engines rested, and high freeboards — hull areas above water — and were strongly built so that they went deep into the water. This was exactly *wrong* for the conditions, and by 1850 builders had learned two major lessons: to minimize the boat's dead weight and to distribute it widely rather than deeply.

The classic Western River boat had a broad, shallow hull with an absolutely flat bottom, and the contents of the boat went *on* it rather than *in* it. The main deck was only a few feet — sometimes only a few inches — above the water, and carried boilers, fuel, engines, cargo, and a motley group of deckhands, firemen, and deck passengers who staked out whatever territory they could find. Above these, reached by a stair from the bow, was the "boiler deck," with a long cabin lined with staterooms for the moneyed passengers. Forward were the purser's office, the bar, and the rooms for single men; aft, in a somewhat taboo area signaled by carpet rather than spitoons, was the "ladies' cabin" for women

The Caledonia, *a Western River boat of 1823, is still equipped with seagoing features of its time: a hull high out of the water and a bluff bow with a bowsprit, heavy cutwater, and trailboards.*

and married couples. Above, usually, was the "texas," the officers' deckhouse, with the pilothouse riding on top. This, of course, was on a large packet; there were other steamboats, smaller and simpler ones, and ones for other purposes.

Construction was light, pieced together with slender timbers, boards, and iron rods. The hull was crisscrossed with partitions and trusswork, and further trusswork went through and above the upper decks to keep the whole flimsy ensemble of scantlings and boards in shape. It was usual for a boat to have a "sheer," an upward curve toward either end. This was partly a matter of aesthetics — it gave the boat a graceful, advancing look — and partly a practical matter of breasting the river's few small waves or raising a sternwheel to give its buckets the proper "dip" for driving the boat. Hog chains, iron rods supported by a fanned-out group of wooden braces, maintained this sheer, and there were other posts, braces, and iron rods crosswise to hold up the main deck.

Such a boat needed a special kind of engine, and by 1850 it had been provided. Fulton had used a low-pressure Watt and Boulton engine on the *North River Boat of Clermont*; it was a product of the English makers who had first used steam as a working fluid and who were among the first to make an engine that could turn some-

The Louisville and Cincinnati Mail Line sidewheeler Jacob Strader, *1856, shows the classic Western River packet type.*

Western River engine, c.1900, built by James Rees & Sons Company of Pittsburgh. This is a "simple" engine, expanding its steam in a single pressure range. Part of the wooden pitman, the connecting rod to the sternwheel, is shown to the right above the massive cylinder timber "W."

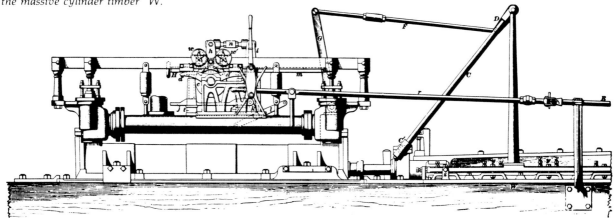

thing. But a more compact engine, using higher-pressure steam, was needed to drive Western River boats against flood currents and over shoals while saving on weight and space, and the distinctive Western River engine was the answer.

European engineers, and even engineers from the Eastern Seaboard, regarded these engines with contempt, pity, or stupefaction; yet they were exactly what was needed. Strange contraptions of levers and rods, lucid as an insurance policy to the uninformed, their gangling forms lacked the tight, heavy-boned look of conventional marine engines. They seemed to sprawl on the heavy timbers that supported them, and except for the heavy pitmans, the connecting rods that actually turned the wheels, they seemed a little too small for their job. But the lightness and looseness was essential. The up-and-down driving of a conventional marine engine would have racked the hull even worse than ordinary river service already did; the slow and more or less horizontal motion of the Western River

engine was kinder to its timbers. Again, the hull itself would always sag and warp, and the loose-jointed engine could adjust to this. Finally, its strung-out anatomy eased the making, adjustment, servicing, and replacement of parts.

(continued on page 26)

George Fitch, a Victorian expert on the Western River boat, said that it ***"must be so built that when the river is low and the sandbars come out for air, the first mate can tap a keg of beer and run the boat four miles on the suds."***
Also, that *"if a steamboat should go to sea, the ocean would take one playful slap at it, and people would be picking up kindling on the beach for the next eleven years."*

The limberness of wooden steamboat construction is evident in this photograph of the Combine towboat Jim Wood, *washed up on the guide wall of a lock in 1917. Unlike some other boats in this situation, the* Jim Wood *did not survive.*

Charles Dickens in Pittsburgh

When the British author Charles Dickens (1812-1870) came to Pittsburgh in 1842, he was already a celebrity, with *Pickwick Papers, Oliver Twist, Nicholas Nickleby,* and *The Old Curiosity Shop* to his credit. The United States both intrigued and annoyed Dickens, as his *American Notes for General Circulation* shows clearly. His annoyance is caustically expressed as well in the American episodes of *Martin Chuzzlewit,* published in 1843. Here are two passages from *American Notes:*

On the Monday evening, furnace fires and clanking hammers on the banks of the [Pennsylvania] canal warned us that we approached the termination of this part of our journey. After going through another dreamy place — a long aqueduct across the Alleghany [sic] River, which was stranger than the bridge at Harrisburg, being a vast, low, wooden chamber full of water — we emerged upon that ugly confusion of backs of buildings, and crazy galleries and stairs, which always abuts on water, whether it be river, sea, canal, or ditch: and were at Pittsburg [sic].

Pittsburg is like Birmingham in England; at least, its townspeople say so. Setting aside the streets, the shops, the houses, wagons, factories, public buildings, and population, perhaps it may be.

It certainly has a great quantity of smoke hanging about it, and is famous for its iron-works. . . . It is very beautifully situated on the Alleghany River, over which there are two bridges; and the villas of the wealthier citizens, sprinkled about the high grounds in the neighborhood, are pretty enough. We lodged at a most excellent hotel, and were admirably served. As usual, it was full of boarders, was very large, and had a broad colonnade to every story of the house. □

This is Pittsburgh just about the time when Dickens was here. The date is established by the presence of the second Courthouse, with its dome, built in 1841, and of the first Smithfield Street Bridge, burned in the fire of 1845.

> *"These western vessels are . . . foreign to all the ideas we are accustomed to entertain of boats."*

He departed for the West by steamboat:

The Messenger was one among a crowd of high-pressure steamboats clustered together by the wharfside, which, looked down upon from the rising ground that forms the landing-place [at Pittsburgh] . . . appeared no larger than so many floating models. . . .

These western vessels are . . . foreign to all the ideas we are accustomed to entertain of boats. I hardly know what to liken them to, or how to describe them.

In the first place, they have no mast, cordage, tackle, rigging, or other such boat-like gear; nor have they anything in their shape at all calculated to remind one of a boat's head, stern, sides, or keel. Except that they are in the water, and display a couple of paddle-boxes, they might be intended, for anything that appears to the contrary, to perform some unknown service, high and dry, upon a mountain-top. There is no visible deck even: nothing but a long, black, ugly roof, covered with burnt-out feathery sparks; above which tower two iron chimneys, and a hoarse escape valve, and a glass steerage house. Then, in order as the eye descends towards the water, are the sides, and doors, and windows of the staterooms, jumbled as oddly together as though they formed a small street, built by the varying tastes of a dozen men: the whole is supported on beams and pillars resting on a dirty barge, but a few inches above the water's edge: and in the narrow space between this upper structure and this barge's deck are the furnace fires and machinery, open at the sides to every wind that blows, and every storm of rain it drives along its path. □

Charles Dickens came to Pittsburgh via the Pennsylvania Canal system, actually a composite: rail from Philadelphia to Columbia on the Susquehanna; canal up that river and the Juniata to Hollidaysburg; Portage Railroad (which carried the canal boats) from there to Johnstown; canal down the Conemaugh, Kiskiminetas, and west shore of the Allegheny to the North Side; then by aqueduct and tunnel through Pittsburgh to the bank of the Monongahela. In the 1830s and '40s, other canals flourished to the north and the west in Pennsylvania.

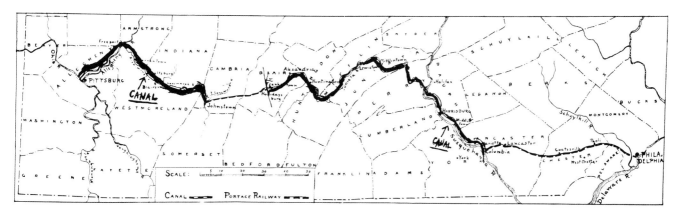

(continued from page 23)

Moored alongside the Ohio River Museum at Marietta is the *W. P. Snyder Jr.*, the last surviving steam towboat on the Upper Ohio, built in 1918 and a good example of a boat visible around Pittsburgh into the mid-1950s. Its two main engines are tandem compounds: that is, each expands the same steam in two pressure ranges, using a smaller and a larger cylinder with a common piston rod. They are by James Rees & Sons Company, the famous Pittsburgh boat builders, and have the Rees variable cutoff that helped economize on steam.

In a Western River boat like the *Snyder*, the engineer got his "bells" — orders from the pilot-house — literally by bell. Like many Upper Ohio towboats, the *Snyder* has four of them, three mounted on spiral springs like Victorian shop bells and one (known on the river as a gong) tapped with a clapper that was tripped. The engineer had to know each of them, interpret its ringing in context, and ring the bell himself — each had a speaking tube to the pilothouse — to show that he understood. If the stopping bell rang while the boat was running, he stopped the

James Rees & Sons Company had its shops (left) directly up the Allegheny from the old Exposition Buildings at the Point, about where the approaches to the Fort Duquesne Bridge are now. In the erecting shop (lower left), the prefabricated steamers were laboriously fitted together to make sure that everything did fit. This is the Colombian steamer Ayacucho of 1921, with its starboard engine being assembled to the left and its doctor pump in the background. Rees boats found their way to strange places, including the rivers of Nigeria, Egypt, and Russia. The Victor von Grot (below) went between Kiakhta, Siberia, and Urga (now Ulan Bator), Mongolia. The Tres Hermanos (bottom) is shown on the Monongahela in 1885, with splashboards already up to fight the waves of the Gulf of Mexico on its delivery run to its Mexican owners.

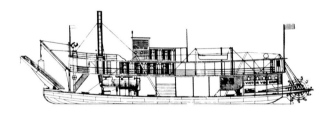

engines; if it rang while they were stopped, he sent them full speed ahead. If the backing bell rang while the boat was running, he went slow in the same direction; if it rang while the boat was stopped, he went full speed astern; if it rang twice, he went slow astern. If the ship-up gong rang once while the engines were stopped, he prepared to reverse: pulled the gear that pulled the chain that rotated the drum that pulled the chains that raised the levers that controlled the poppet valves; pulled the lever that raised or lowered the ship-up jack that held the spider that engaged and disengaged the rocker pins that controlled the wipers; dropped the poppet-valve levers back on the wipers; and obeyed the following bell for steam. If the ship-up gong rang once while running, he gave the engines half-speed in the same direction; if it rang twice, it meant an emergency. If it rang three times, it meant, "Stand by" or else, "Finished with engines." If the chestnut bell rang along with one

or more other bells it meant, "Dead slow" in the way indicated. There were other bell signals for various speeds and directions, involving combinations of up to three bells. On other rivers, the system was different, and the chestnut bell itself was an Upper Ohio feature entirely.

Besides tending the main engines, the engineer of the *Snyder* had to mind the "doctor," or pump that fed water to the boilers; the condenser that turned used steam into warm feedwater; the apparatus that clarified "make-up" feedwater drawn from the river; the dynamo, with its engine; the refrigeration equipment; the steam-powered steering engine; and various other applications of steam, water, and electricity around the boat. On a sidewheeler, he and another engineer would have been responsible for two main engines, turning independently and needing to be kept from stopping on a "dead center," a position at the end of a stroke in which the engine was helpless.

The W. P. Snyder Jr., built in 1918, was a "pool" towboat, with pilothouse and stacks built low to get under the bridges that crossed the pools of dammed water around Pittsburgh. She is now moored alongside the Ohio River Museum at Marietta

Everyone admitted that the Western River packet, carrying people and goods to the new western states, was a powerful instrument of progress and national unification, especially before the railroads were important. And there *was* glamour, for the boiler-deck passengers at least. But it was curious: owners displayed pride in their boats, decorated them in a flamboyant, budget-reckless way. And yet, in their hearts, they wrote them off four or five years in the future. Too much was likely to go wrong. The strains of hard driving, groundings, and landings against raw riverbanks when hailed from the shore were bad enough, but there were serious accidents to fear as well. A boat bottom of thin planks was moving over water in which snags — flood-loosened, waterlogged trees — were reaching like vindictive ghosts with dead roots and limbs. A superstructure of thin boards was illuminated at night with many open flames. Engineers, many of them sketchily trained and none too responsible, were making and using high-pressure steam in roughly-made contrivances. Sometimes a boiler could be seen to "pant" with each engine stroke; sometimes the engineer put too much weight on the "death hook" at the end of the lever that held down the safety valve; sometimes he absent-mindedly let the doctor stop pumping, so that the boiler's dried-out inside began to glow and melt, then started it up again and released a jet of water onto the boiler's soft, red-hot surfaces. Charles Dickens, visiting Pittsburgh in 1842, was advised to take a stateroom astern, in the ladies' cabin, since "steamboats generally blew up forward." Mrs. Dickens was along, so he had that privilege. Gradually, legislation, technology, and the work of the Army Corps of Engineers made river travel much less hazardous, yet accidents still happen now and then; they always will.

The glamour boat of the Western Rivers was the sidewheeler, with its huge paddle boxes that proudly bore the names of the boat and its owners, and possibly a decorative painting as

The Pittsburgh & Cincinnati sternwheel packet Virginia *was one of the proudest boats on the Upper Ohio; but on one stormy night, during a subsiding flood, Captain William L. Anderson tried to land a passenger and ended up stranded in a cornfield. Here, tourists have come by a specially-scheduled B&O excursion train to witness the unusual sight. The* Virginia *was eventually moved to the river and floated off.*

well. Its hull, relatively slender because of the great width the paddlewheels demanded, had "fast" lines, and the modest speed records of the Western Rivers — somewhere around 15 miles an hour — were made by sidewheelers.

The sternwheeler was a homelier boat, a wagon beside the sidewheeler's chariot. And yet it was the sternwheeler that prevailed, for much the same reason that on the sea the clipper vanished after two or three decades of glory while the bulkier and slower barque kept on. In each case, where speed was wanted something faster became available, and the slower, more economical vessel had more of a chance. Once railroads began to run parallel to the rivers, as they did late in the nineteenth century, people and freight in a hurry went by rail.

To be sure, the grandest of all the sidewheelers appeared on the Lower Mississippi in the decade or so after the Civil War. But the *J. M. White* and the *Robert E. Lee* were cotton boats, serving their purpose best as fantastic, flammable masses of stacked-up bales with only the pilot-house and the smokestacks visible above, heading for New Orleans.

For people and goods where speed was unimportant, the sternwheeler sufficed. The placing of its engines aft cleared deck and cabin space amidships. The placing of the wheel beyond the hull eliminated a great inherent vice of the sidewheeler, the slap of the paddles against the water that sent rhythmic shocks through the center of the boat, unnerving the passengers and fatiguing the structure. Finally, it economized on engineering crew, since its two engines acted as one. Once the problems of making powerful enough boilers and engines, and of devising trusswork that would keep the heavy sternwheel above the water had been resolved, the ambling sternwheeler became increasingly important. Sidewheelers held on, here and there, for decades, and the sidewheel excursion boat *Senator* — big, old, and gingerbread-hung — called at Pittsburgh until World War II. □

Built in 1883, the sidewheeler Senator *was a mammoth excursion boat that visited Pittsburgh every summer in the years before World War II.*

Victorian Pittsburgh

Pittsburgh in 1859, in a lithographic view by William Schuchman. On the waterfront, shown as crowded with boats, the sidewheeler still predominates, but sternwheelers large and small are beginning to appear. Two flatboats drift down the Monongahela, and a raft seems to be heading in for a landing on the Allegheny. The first bridge up the Allegheny, like the first up the Monongahela, is a suspension bridge by the famous engineer John Roebling. The second Courthouse (far right) shares with the second St. Paul's Cathedral the domination of a scene of industrial and commercial buildings, most of them modest in size. In the background, up the Allegheny, the latticed iron trusses of the Pittsburgh, Fort Wayne & Chicago Railway have replaced the Pennsylvania Canal aqueduct; canal traffic is close to extinction, and the railroad is beginning its time of vigorous growth. After the Civil War that is to start the following year, the packets will begin to decrease in number, though even in 1930 there will still be a handful. But increasingly, the Pittsburgh waterfront will be crowded with towboats and barges moving coal, not passengers and freight.

IEW OF PITTSBURGH, PA.

The Queen City

When the *Queen City* was brought out in 1897, she was one of the best boats on the Upper Ohio: a stern-wheel packet built for comfort rather than speed on the 470-mile run between Pittsburgh and Cincinnati. The idea of boat travel purely for pleasure, reflected in the advertisement below, was not a new idea in the 1890s. There were excursion boats already, and packets were taking northerners to the New Orleans Mardi Gras by the 1880s. The *Queen City* was the first packet to offer Mardi Gras trips from Pittsburgh, beginning in 1903, and made them for many years. She was retired in the early 1940s, served briefly as a wharf boat at Pittsburgh, then was intentionally burned, 45 years old, after suffering flood damage.

The Queen City *(above) at the New Orleans wharf during the 1925 Mardi Gras, with the* Cincinnati *to the right. Captain Edgar E. Brookhart (middle) in the pilothouse; and the* Queen City *officers on deck (bottom).*

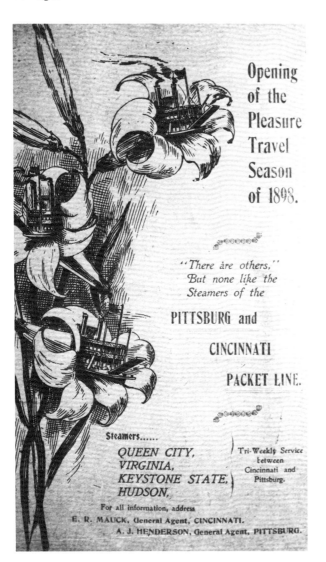

Opening
of the
Pleasure
Travel
Season
of 1898.

"*There are others,*"
But none like the
Steamers of the

PITTSBURG and

CINCINNATI

PACKET LINE.

Steamers......

QUEEN CITY,
VIRGINIA,
KEYSTONE STATE,
HUDSON,

Tri-Weekly Service
between
Cincinnati and
Pittsburg.

For all information, address
E. R. MAUCK, General Agent, CINCINNATI.
A. J. HENDERSON, General Agent, PITTSBURG.

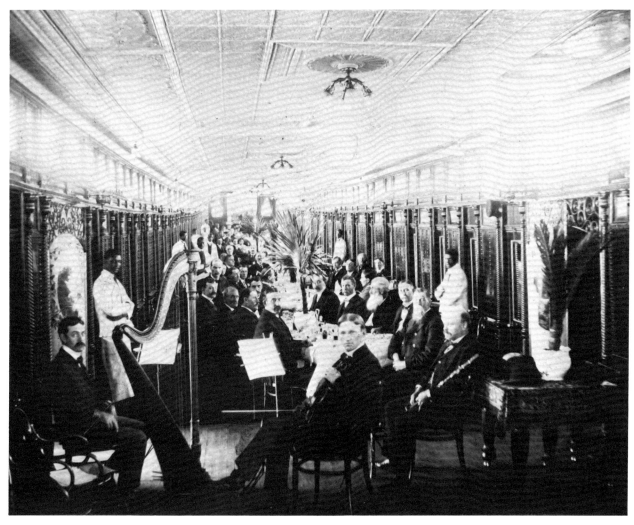

The saloon of the Queen City, c.1900: varnished wood-work, pressed-metal ceiling, occasional electroliers. The women dine astern, the men forward near an orchestra consisting of harp, violin, and clarinet.

THE TOWBOAT

The packet was suited for carrying packages, crates, bales, and barrels as well as passengers, but not for bulk cargoes. These could drift downstream in flatboats or coalboats, and this was satisfactory as long as no large amount of bulk cargo was coming north. Coal was being floated down the Monongahela in the 1780s, and down the Ohio to Anthony Wayne's troops in 1793. Commercial coal shipments to Louisville began in 1814, and Pittsburgh-area coal was going all the way to New Orleans by 1830. As had been usual with flatboats, the coalboats used were broken up and sold as lumber once they were unloaded.

Sometime in the 1830s, though, steamers began the practice of moving keelboats, lashed alongside, upstream and down, and by 1855 a distinct type of steamboat, the towboat, had evolved to move barges in groups. In essence, the towboat was the engine and rudder for a large composite vessel made up of itself and its barges. "Push towing," practical in waters free of high waves, soon became standard. The tow-

"Making Up a Tow by Searchlight at Pittsburgh"; Harper's Weekly, June 14, 1890.

Towboats along the Monongahela wharf at Pittsburgh, c.1900. The sternwheelers are typical: prominent hog trusses to keep the wooden hulls in shape, 'scape pipes over the engine rooms to release exhaust steam, stacks with tackle to lower their tops when passing under bridges. Across the river, to the left, is the first part of the P&LE trainshed, and next to it the freight house. (This area is now Station Square.) The present terminal building was not built until 1901. To the right is the residential-industrial neighborhood of Limerick.

boat pilot, eyes forward toward a flag on the foremost barge in the dead-ahead direction, dominated a tightly-bound mass of rectangular hulls that moved as a single rigid entity.

Maneuvering the tow was a challenge: threading it along whatever channel the stage of water afforded, keeping it clear of the bridge piers that could smash one frail wooden barge after another and deposit the loads like sacrifices at their foundations. The towboats were sternwheelers, with three to five rudders ahead of the wheel and only rarely any astern of it. This meant that when the boat was going ahead the jet of water from the sternwheel was wasted as a help in turning. It was long the custom to put the boat as far astern of the barges as possible, leaving a "duckpond" space ahead of it, to get maximum leverage to turn the whole mass. On especially tight curves, too, the pilot resorted to "flanking"; he simply had the engines reversed, so that the wheel dashed water against the rudders to maximize their turning force. The maneuver is still used.

It was Pittsburgh coal that really got towing started, and it was to be an increasing presence on the rivers. Shortly after 1900 the Monongahela River Consolidated Coal and Coke company (the "Combine"), an industrial giant in an age of giants, owned 63 percent of *all* Western River tonnage: 80 towboats and 4,000 barges, coalboats, and other craft. Pittsburgh waterfront scenes often show the Combine's RC symbol on pilothouses, barges, and wharfboats. ☐

A tow moves down the Allegheny under the Fort Wayne railroad bridge, in the years before urban renewal changed the character of the central North Side.

On September 30, 1908, Pittsburgh celebrated its Ses-quicentennial. In this marine parade, wooden sternwheel towboats head, two by two, down the Ohio past Manchester. In the foreground, wooden coal barges await their turn to be moved away. In their midst is a pump boat, used to keep the barges dry. The nearest towboat and all the moored craft are marked "RC," the symbol of the Combine.

ENGINEERING THE RIVERS

The first river in Pennsylvania to be declared officially navigable was, oddly enough, the Kiskiminetas. The Kiski is quite a modest river, not an obvious highway of commerce, yet the Pennsylvania Council's ordinance of 1771 was intended to protect it, with some such role in mind, from man-made obstructions. Toward the end of the eighteenth century, the State of Pennsylvania became further interested in the navigability of Western Pennsylvania streams and had quite a lot done in the way of picking up rocks and dead trees from Allegheny and Monongahela tributaries and preventing their obstruction by trash and man-made works. The Conemaugh, which is simply the name of the Kiski at its Johnstown point of origin, became something of a starting point for southbound flatboats. French Creek became a coalboat-building place and a flatboat route, and was canalized to Meadville in 1834. The Youghiogheny, which also benefited from the cleaning-up process, was never as important.

The early navigators had no real U.S. government help until 1824, when Congress passed the first Inland Waterways Improvement Act, giving responsibility for keeping the Ohio navigable to the U.S. Army Corps of Engineers. Early efforts were directed against snags and sandbars. Snag boats ripped up the dead trees with great beaks, then hauled them aboard for sawing up; training dikes, jutting from the shores, concentrated the current to wash away the piled-up sand that the eddying river had deposited.

Water continued to flow down the river in the same fluctuating way, though, and the Ohio could be forded at times in the summer. In

"The New Government Work at Davis Island Dam"; Frank Leslie's Illustrated Newspaper, October 16, 1880.
1. The Ohio during low water. 2. River and Dam during high water. 3. Working Model of the Dam. 4. The Coffer-dam for the Land Wall. 5. Constructing the Land Wall.

droughts, steamers and barges might virtually pave the Monongahela at Pittsburgh, waiting for high enough water to take them where they were bound. Dams were needed to keep the river level high, and in 1885 the first of those on the Ohio was completed at Davis Island, about five miles down from the Point. It was a "Chanoine wicket" dam, a wall of trapdoors that rose from the riverbed when water was low. At such times vessels would use a lock to one side; when the river was full, the wickets would lie flat and the vessels would pass over them as if they were not there.

Once in the dam-building business, the Engineers stayed in it, building and rebuilding until the entire Ohio was "canalized," turned into a series of step-like pools of deep, quiet water. The result of a grand construction campaign begun in 1910, the Ohio canalization was officially declared complete on October 18, 1929, just before the stock-market crash, on an occasion of whistle-blowing triumph at Pittsburgh's Monongahela Wharf.

Celebrating the "canalization" of the Ohio River; October 18, 1929.

The Emsworth Locks and Dams, six miles down the Ohio from the Pittsburgh Point. Completed in 1921 as part of the canalization project, Emsworth was transformed in 1938 to the form seen here, with adjustable gates to maintain a pool level of 710 feet above sea level between here and the dams at Highland Park and Braddock.

The Monongahela after 1836 was virtually a proprietary river, with toll locks and dams owned by the financially sickly Monongahela Navigation Company. In 1897, after a legal fight, the United States took over the system and handed it over to the Engineers, who eventually rebuilt it completely and canalized the river to its end at Fairmont, West Virginia.

The Allegheny, never a major towboat river despite its volume of water, was canalized as far as East Brady, 72 miles up, mainly in a campaign of the 1930s.

The Falls of the Ohio, at Louisville, were long an annoyance to navigators. Louisville enjoyed the situation well enough because its people were hired as pilots through the "chutes" of deeper water and to transship goods from boats above to boats below; but Pittsburgh, Wheeling, Cincinnati, and other Upper Ohio ports were less appreciative. In 1830 a private toll canal, the Louisville and Portland, opened, but proved a bottleneck for packets as they increased in size. A good many of the steamers on the Upper Ohio always stayed there, and those designed to go through the locks were awkward and uneconomical affairs, made to give the maximum payload under the circumstances. Large builder's boats from Pittsburgh had to go, riskily, down the chutes on their delivery runs. In 1872 the canal was rebuilt for modern demands, and has been rebuilt since for the largest present-day tows. □

"At last, out of bondage." As an operator of private locks and dams, the Monongahela Navigation Company had virtually owned the Monongahela River from 1836 and had not done particularly well by anyone, including itself, in the process. Litigation finally put the system in the hands of the federal government in 1897, and the Army Corps of Engineers began the task of reconstruction and new construction to meet modern needs. Here, boatmen are celebrating the takeover.

A NEW KIND OF BOAT

The dogged work of the Army Engineers in canalizing the rivers and clearing them of debris and obstacles encouraged the replacement of the steam sternwheel towboat by the diesel propeller boats that are standard today. Propellers were in use at sea from 1840 on, but until the channels were clear of objects that they might strike, they were not practical on the rivers. A paddlewheel "bucket" was just a plank, and if it broke on something it could easily be unbolted and replaced. If a blade or a shaft broke on a propeller boat, the boat was helpless and had to go to a boatyard for long, expensive repairs. Canalization, combined with flood-control measures that left potential flotsam untouched on the shores, reduced the hazard greatly.

The diesel engine had appeared in its first practical form in 1897, offering the high rotative speeds the propeller needed while being compact and free of the heavy, hull-racking thrust of a steam propeller engine. The diesel, though, did demand a hull of steel, light enough to draw less than the nine feet of water the Engineers' channel guaranteed yet strong enough to take the engine's weight and vibration. River operators had long been leery of metal hulls, mainly because of their high first cost though partly perhaps because boat-building was traditionally a woodworking affair and it was in wood that the skills of the proven builders lay. The iron-hulled *Valley Forge*, built at Pittsburgh in 1839, got some praise but little imitation, and though the Pittsburgh engine builder James Rees & Sons Company fabricated many iron and steel boats late in the century for the government and for foreign customers, local private operators remained cool. In 1905, 19 out of 20 Western River boats were still made entirely of wood.

Out of a slow evolution that included chain-driven diesel-powered sternwheelers came a few diesel propeller boats by the early 1930s. The discovery of the Kort nozzle in 1937 by a Dravo

Stern of a modern towboat. In the foreground are the four flanking rudders, then the propellers inside their Kort nozzles, then the two steering rudders.

executive in Germany completed the process. The nozzle, a shrouding designed to lessen the erosive effects on riverbanks by concentrating propeller wash, also turned out to give the propellers 25 percent more thrust. That did it. In 1940 the *Jason,* the last steam sternwheeler for Upper Ohio service, was launched, and after the war the towboats we see today became standard. Steam disappeared from the Pittsburgh area around 1955, and the diesel sternwheelers, all little boats, have quietly disappeared as well. □

The Sam Craig *was built in 1929. This last type of steam towboat, steel-hulled, could almost do without the visible hog trusses of the wooden boats.*

Bridges

Bridges are conspicuous from the river, yet paradoxically they are ways of ignoring the river. In the Port of Pittsburgh, there are 19 main-channel spans on the Allegheny, 24 on the Monongahela, and 11 on the Ohio; these 54 are perhaps a fortieth of the total number in this up-and-down region of ours, but they are among the biggest and most easily seen.

The Fort Pitt Bridge (left), built in 1958, is the city's most dramatic gateway. As traffic emerges from the Fort Pitt Tunnel, the city across the Monongahela appears suddenly, framed in the bridge's arches and cables.

The Smithfield Street Bridge (middle), an early work of steel construction from 1883, shows a Victorian approach to engineering: limber trusses, assembled from many small pieces.

When the river's surface is unruffled, an illusory arch appears in the water (bottom).

In memoriam: the Point before the "Pittsburgh Renaissance," with the Point Bridge of 1927 (foreground) and the Manchester Bridge of 1915 converging on a rudimentary Point Park.

John Augustus Roebling (1806-1869)

Roebling designed the second Sixth Street Bridge in 1859. He was the grand master of the suspension bridge and the first American manufacturer of the wire cable that eased its construction. This is one of three suspension bridges he built in Pittsburgh, two of them while living in Saxonburg near by. The others were an aqueduct of 1845 for the Pennsylvania Canal and the Smithfield Street Bridge of 1846, replaced in the early 1880s by the present one. Later, Roebling was to design the Brooklyn Bridge in New York City.

Union Bridge, 1874. It is odd to think of an ironmaking city getting a wooden covered bridge at such a late date, but Pittsburgh did. Its five low-clearance spans frustrated river operators until 1907, when it was demolished. Of its successor, the Manchester Bridge, nothing now remains but the portal sculptures, which are at the Old Post Office Museum on Pittsburgh's North Side, and various steel embellishments now on display at Bessemer Court in Station Square.

The Virginia *was the first boat to go under the Wabash Railroad Bridge over the Monongahela when completed in 1904 to the designs of Boller and Hodge. Today only supporting piers of this great bridge remain, one near Stanwix Street, one near the Sheraton at Station Square. The distance from pier to pier, 812 feet, suggests the scale on which the Wabash Pittsburgh Terminal Railway Company facilities in the Triangle were built. The whole enterprise failed, not least because the bridge, big as it was, was a traffic bottleneck. In the late 1920s it carried only six passenger trains a day. The trainshed was burned in a fire in 1946, and the grandiose terminal building was demolished in the mid-1950s.*

The West End Bridge was erected between 1930 and 1932 by the Allegheny County Department of Works. Like a triumphal gateway, the 755-foot tied arch of the West End Bridge spans the Ohio a mile down from the Point. The County, in a massive building campaign of the late 1920s, designed and built some of the most graceful and progressive bridges in the nation, and this may be its masterpiece.

THE TOWBOAT TODAY

An old technology tends to gather nostalgia around it as it fades away. People's pasts are involved with it; some worked with it, others knew it as bystanders, in whose lives it was a background element. It must have had a lot in the way of inefficiency, annoyance, or danger for people to be willing to forget it.

As a technology progresses, it tends to lose a certain drama it once had. Old machinery, old engineering works are apt to be visual essays in opposing forces, to show in a multitude of exposed parts how they were built and how they work. The newer versions, in being more efficient, are more compact, more secretive, more the neutrally-packaged thing that an industrial designer can "style." Think of the contrasts in towboats in a few decades: the big red sternwheel, tossing up a glittering bustle of water, versus the propellers whose wakes are all that announce the boat's driving force; the Western River engine, stretching and folding itself with a rumble and a swish perhaps 15 times a minute, versus the roaring, encased diesel going at 900 revolutions per minute; the twin pipe-like stacks

This sight was a familiar one into the mid-1950s: a sternwheeler, with water cascading from its wheel, going up the Monongahela past the P&LE Station.

that emitted billows of boiler smoke versus the styled, oversized stacks, like overturned wastebaskets, that shroud the pipes from which the diesel fumes jet; the old engine room, where the engineer pulled on his controls as the bells jangled, versus control of the engines from the pilothouse to the hiss of pneumatic clutches; the whistle that announced the presence of the steamer with solemn organ notes echoing from the hillsides versus the electric air horn, itself a vestigial formality on a boat with radio and radar for safe navigation; the very construction: planks on wooden scantlings versus steel plate welded to structural shapes.

The modern towboat, though, has a look of confidence. It is built with certain work in mind, and it does this efficiently, safely. Its neutral forms lack drama, but they imply the growing perfection of the boat itself. Drama usually means waste and risk; lack of drama suggests that things are under control.

Compared with those of the Lower Mississippi, towing operations in the Port of Pittsburgh area are modest. The *Sprague*, mightiest of the sternwheelers with an estimated 2,700 horsepower, came to Pittsburgh only twice as an active towboat; her power was wasted here. And the most powerful of the Lower Mississippi towboats today, three screws and 10,500 horsepower, capable of pushing 60,000 tons on 40 barges, may be built here but once they go downriver they never return. Our present limit is around 6,000 horsepower, twin screws, and up to 15 barges. This is an impressive sight in itself, to be sure. A typical barge is 195 feet long and 35 feet wide, and for passing through the Ohio River locks a tow of such barges is made up five long and three across. This is an area 975 feet long and 105 feet wide; add to this a towboat 160 or 170 feet long, and you have an object nearly 1,150 feet long that the pilot is maneuvering around the tight bends of the Lower Monongahela, between the closely-spaced Pittsburgh bridge piers, and eventually into lock chambers very slightly bigger than the tow itself.

The great old towboat Sprague *came north from its retirement place at Vicksburg for the Pittsburgh Bicentennial in 1959. Built in 1902, she was 318 feet long with a 40-foot wheel. This was replaced by a smaller wheel with less thrust after the* Sprague *smashed into a showboat on her maiden trip.*

The efficient, precise appearance of a modern pilothouse (top right). This towboat is triple-screw, as the three control levers at the center indicate, and thus of a type rarely seen in the Pittsburgh area. To either side are levers for the steering and flanking rudders.

A 15-barge tow, the largest seen on Western Pennsylvania waters (bottom right). This is small beside the 40-barge Lower Mississippi tows, but even so is about 1,150 feet long by 105 feet wide.

Of course, towboats come in many sizes. There are tiny workboats of about 700 horsepower that have a function equivalent to that of a switch engine in a railroad yard, pushing an individual barge or two for short distances or helping make up a tow for the boat that will move it. Beyond these, there are boats suitable for the smaller tows of the Upper Monongahela and the Allegheny, and for short hauls in the Port of Pittsburgh area. Finally, there are the boats meant to take the 15-barge maximum as far as Cairo, where it may be put into a larger Mississippi tow in charge of a more powerful boat. One of the largest boats in present use here, twin-screw and 5,600 horsepower, is characterized in this succinct way by Cornelis van Mook, a naval architect for Dravo Corporation:

Typically, these vessels carry a crew of 11, made up of captain, pilot, chief engineer, engineer, mate, watchman, four deckhands, and one cook. There is a spare room for service mechanics, electronics repairmen, etc. Many boats have a bedroom and a sitting room on the texas deck used only for guests of the owner.

The boat holds 64,000 gallons of diesel fuel, enough for about 10 to 14 days. At $1.05/gallon for diesel fuel, it takes more than an oil company credit card to refuel. The boat holds 14,200 gallons of fresh water, which will be used at a rate of 1,000 to 1,100 gallons per day by a crew of 11.

All personnel stand two watches per day, six hours on, six hours off, except the cook. Watches change at 6:00 and 12:00. Meals are served in two sittings of one half hour each, starting on the half hour before the watch change and ending on the half hour after.

The cook gets up at 4:30 a.m. to make breakfast for the 5:30 to 6:30 a.m. breakfast sittings. Lunch is from 11:30 to 12:30 and dinner is from 5:30 to 6:30 p.m. She (or he) should be in bed by 8:30 p.m.

The captain and pilot take their turns steering the boat, while the engineers take turns minding the machinery.

The mate (really a boatswain in sea parlance) is in charge of two deckhands to mind the tow on one watch. The watchman and the two other deckhands do the same on the other watch.

Generally, the crew will work 30 to 35 days, seven days a week, on the boat. A relief crew then takes over while the original crew is off for 30 to 35 days.

The crew is closely knit; they must get along with each other, and they are a proud lot who take good care of the boat and each other. The boat is their home half the year, and they live together as a family while on board. □

A workboat, having about 700 horsepower and used for moving a barge or two short distances.

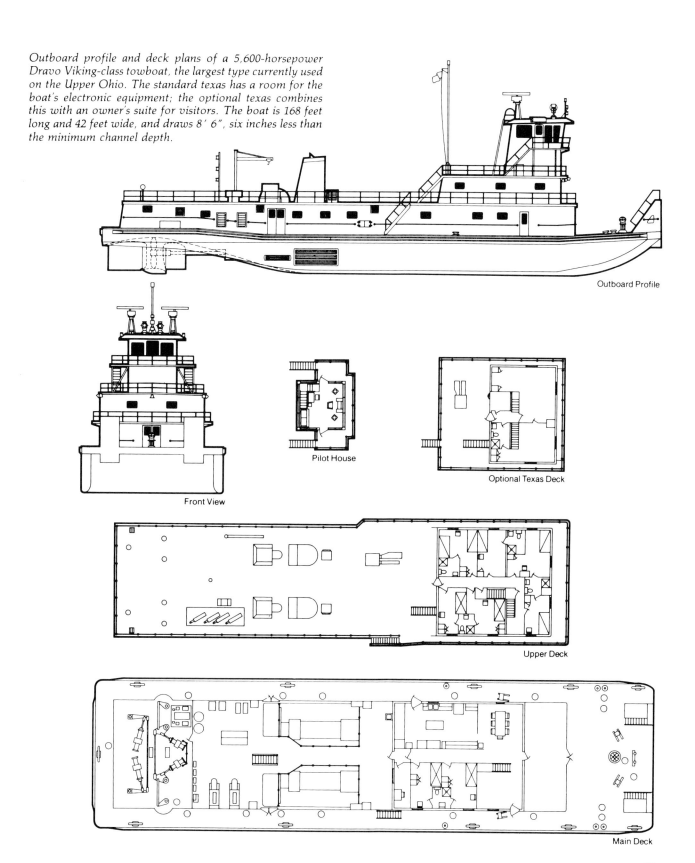

Outboard profile and deck plans of a 5,600-horsepower
Dravo Viking-class towboat, the largest type currently used
on the Upper Ohio. The standard texas has a room for the
boat's electronic equipment; the optional texas combines
this with an owner's suite for visitors. The boat is 168 feet
long and 42 feet wide, and draws 8' 6", six inches less than
the minimum channel depth.

Outboard Profile

Front View

Pilot House

Optional Texas Deck

Upper Deck

Main Deck

51

BARGES

If the towboat has a look of quiet competence, the barge is more of a stoic, taking whatever fate offers it with resignation. The builder sends it sideways into the water in a plain but handsome deep-red color, varied with a few informative numerals and legends in white; but after that it seldom knows the touch of new paint and pursues most of its career in a vague rusty hue. If need be, its owner can find out at any moment where it is and what it is doing, but otherwise it is exactly like a freight car in its useful anonymity. On a trip to New Orleans, it will be handed on from boat to boat, each boat designed for the size of tow to be expected in a specific stretch of river; like a freight train, the tow will lose and gain barges along the way as shippers claim and consign their cargoes.

Like a railroad car, too, the barge tends to come in standard sizes. Typical is 195 feet by 35 feet by 12 feet deep, dimensions determined by Ohio River lock chambers 1,200 or 600 feet long and 110 feet wide and by a channel nine feet deep. Occasionally, barges are as long as 200 feet, or in special cases more, and barges that go up the Monongahela past the second lock are dimensioned 175 by 26 feet to fit the smaller chambers of that river.

The commonest sort of barge, that heaped with the coal that constitutes about four-fifths of the cargo in the Pittsburgh area, is the open-hopper barge. The hopper is the hold, and it is uncovered, and material unaffected by the weather is dumped in and scooped out repeatedly, and that is the story of this barge's life. Fully loaded, almost slithering on the bottom of the channel, it holds 1,500 tons of material, as much as will load 15 jumbo hopper cars or 60 large tractor-trailers.

Coal, by the way, is of two sorts: steam coal, which has a high sulfur content, and metallurgical coal, suitable for making into coke. Steam coal is strip-mined down the Ohio and up the Monongahela, and goes to power plants along both rivers as well as down the Ohio for export. "Met" coal comes mostly from up the Monongahela and is shipped down to coking plants at various places; some of it is mixed with power-plant steam coal to meet pollution standards. This explains the peculiar sight of one tow of coal crossing another: different sorts from different places for different users.

Covered dry-cargo barges are essentially the same as open-hopper ones in dimensions and capacity, but have corrugated metal hatch covers that slide or are lowered over the hopper to protect the cargo. In the case of the deck barge, the load rides on the barge, not in it. Typical cargoes for a deck barge would be an outsize piece of machinery or structural component, or dredged material being allowed to drain into the river. Tank barges tend to look much like the covered barges, and it is their piping, an occasional small tank on deck, and often a little red flag amidships, symbolizing an inflammable cargo, that show what they are. Rarer but conspicuous when they appear are dredges, maintaining the channel, and floating cranes, on their way to lift something heavy onto a barge or out of the water. Even rarer species turn up now and then.   □

The double-rake coal barge, with a coaming (a raised edge to confine the upper part of the load), is shorter and narrower than those common on the Ohio: 175 by 26 feet, exactly the dimensions of the old-time wooden coalboat.

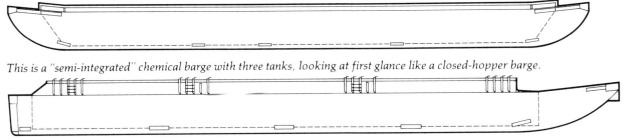

This is a "semi-integrated" chemical barge with three tanks, looking at first glance like a closed-hopper barge.

An "integrated fleet" of tank barges —
four hulls designed to fit together as one
— moves up the Monongahela past
Pittsburgh (below).

NAVIGATION

Navigation of the rivers these days is relatively (not absolutely) safe. Things that can go wrong include: fire on a towboat; a towboat jamming under a bridge through overestimating the clearance in abnormally high water; a badly-moored barge breaking away and perhaps knocking other barges loose (in June 1981, 58 barges got loose this way during a storm); motorboat operators failing to clear the way for a moving tow or getting sucked under it, or even running into a vessel they had no reason not to notice.

What seem like the biggest risks, those of getting a big tow down a channel, are actually the ones that cause the least trouble. A towboat is very maneuverable — it can even "crab," that is, go sideways — and in the slack water around Pittsburgh a tow can usually either stop in one-and-a-half tow lengths or make a complete turn in its own length. Where necessary, pilots take things very slowly, checking ahead by radiotelephone with approaching vessels, scanning the water ahead with their radar. In this they are guided by the Rules of the Road, which prescribe the maneuvers of every type of vessel in any situation where there could be an accident, tell what lights a given sort of vessel is to carry, and what whistle (really, air horn) blasts are to be given — one: "Will pass port to port"; two: "Will pass starboard to starboard"; three: "Am reversing"; one long: "Am starting out" or "Am approaching from around a blind bend."

The Army Engineers and the Coast Guard share the job of making the rivers safe, dependable roadways. The Engineers build and run the locks and dams, establish the extent to which things can be built in or into the water, and maintain the navigation channels by dredging. They also maintain navigational markers in the vicinity of the locks, showing the ways in and out. The Coast Guard does just about everything else: establishes the buoys and lights along the rivers, inspects towboats for safety equipment, inspects all new craft for soundness and all craft carrying hazardous cargo and potential pollutants from time to time, inspects docking facilities, prosecutes perpetrators of oil spills and sees that these are cleaned up, and polices the river generally. Their boats, white-hulled with bright-orange diagonal bands toward the bows, are often to be seen, though except for the buoy tender *Osage* they are small cabin craft. The Coast Guard also works with private boating clubs to preach safety to motorboat operators, water-skiers, and other recreationists who sometimes are not too objective about the hazards of a busy waterway.

In June 1981, during a storm with high water, a barge broke loose from its moorings. Crashing into other moored barges, it broke them loose; they then crashed into other moored barges and broke them loose. In all, 58 barges sped down the river, out of control, hitting bridge piers, and lodging against them. Accidents — though far less frequent than in the old days — are inevitable.

Making sense of the nautical road itself with its navigational markers, however, devolves somehow on the Engineers, whose books of charts show every bit of river deemed commercially navigable. To a seagoing navigator the charts seem primitive: no soundings, since the pilot can assume that he has at least nine feet of water in the channel; no notes on the nature of the riverbed since he is not going to anchor (but will tie up to a tree if he is making an impromptu stop); no notes on tides, no compass roses — not relevant on the rivers. Instead, he will be shown the areas of shoal water, the direction of the current, and the course of the channel. The red buoys on the right side of the channel (facing upstream) and the black buoys on the opposite side will appear in their proper places, as will the water intakes, the cable crossings, the bridges (whose profiles are shown), and the landings (which are identified). All quite simple, though the pilot *will* be expected to make sense of "Line Island Light & Daymark 41.4 Gp. Fl. W., 5 Sec.

2 Flashes, TR, TR" (translated to mean: 41.4 miles down the Ohio from the Pittsburgh Point, a flashing white light, giving groups of two flashes every five seconds; in the daytime, a triangular red daymark with a red reflective border is visible from both directions). □

Numbers 1 through 6 on this page from a book of navigation charts show things crossing the river; letters A through V designate landings and other features along the banks. A hatched square is a commercial dock; an empty square is a recreation dock; a square with "R" in it is a launching ramp. "AP" is an arrival point, a place to wait for signals for going through the locks. The quarter-note symbol is a water intake. In the chart book, the facing pages show profiles and measurements of the bridges and locks.

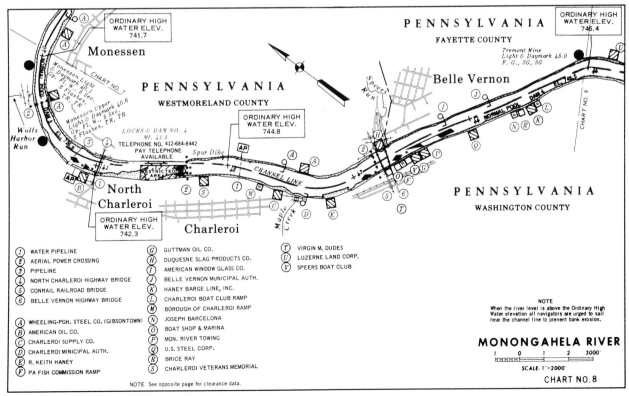

① WATER PIPELINE
② AERIAL POWER CROSSING
③ PIPELINE
④ NORTH CHARLEROI HIGHWAY BRIDGE
⑤ CONRAIL RAILROAD BRIDGE
⑥ BELLE VERNON HIGHWAY BRIDGE

Ⓐ WHEELING-PGH. STEEL CO. (GIBSONTOWN)
Ⓑ AMERICAN OIL CO.
Ⓒ CHARLEROI SUPPLY CO.
Ⓓ CHARLEROI MINICIPAL AUTH.
Ⓔ R. KEITH HANEY
Ⓕ PA FISH COMMISSION RAMP

Ⓖ GUTTMAN OIL CO.
Ⓗ DUQUESNE SLAG PRODUCTS CO.
Ⓘ AMERICAN WINDOW GLASS CO.
Ⓙ BELLE VERNON MUNICIPAL AUTH.
Ⓚ HANEY BARGE LINE, INC.
Ⓛ CHARLEROI BOAT CLUB RAMP
Ⓜ BOROUGH OF CHARLEROI RAMP
Ⓝ JOSEPH BARCELONA
Ⓞ BOAT SHOP & MARINA
Ⓟ MON. RIVER TOWING
Ⓠ U.S. STEEL CORP.
Ⓡ BRICE RAY
Ⓢ CHARLEROI VETERANS MEMORIAL

Ⓣ VIRGIN M. DUDES
Ⓤ LUZERNE LAND CORP.
Ⓥ SPEERS BOAT CLUB

NOTE See opposite page for clearance data.

NOTE
When the river level is above the Ordinary High Water elevation all navigators are urged to sail near the channel line to prevent bank erosion.

MONONGAHELA RIVER

SCALE: 1"=2000'

CHART NO. 8

RIVER ECONOMY

The boats and barges touch shore now and then, at the terminals where they unload and at fleeting areas where tows are made up and broken up. The fleeting areas are the river's equivalent of railroad yards, where little workboats maneuver barges into the right places and the towboat crews, using cables from the boat's capstan and the heavy, T-shaped "ratchets" they carry around the decks, pull them tighter and tighter together. There is nothing much to see on shore at a fleeting area; all the activity is on the water.

The terminals, on the other hand, are apt to be places of heavy machinery, cranes and conveyors, and storage areas for the materials they handle. The forms they take are too many even to begin to describe, from the specialized private terminals to the more versatile public ones for hire to any shipper who can use the facilities they provide.

Barge transportation lacks the glamour of the old river packet, but through it the rivers con-

Two twin-screw boats are under construction here at the Dravo boatyard on Neville Island.

tinue to be a major element in the economy of the Pittsburgh region. Some industries depend absolutely on the water to get their goods in or out, whether because the cheapness of barge transportation helps make their prices competitive or simply because land, in the hill-lined river valleys, is too precious to waste on halted trucks or railroad cars. The Clairton coke works, for example, needs 27,000 tons of coal a day when working at capacity. Twenty-five barges, brought down the Monongahela, supply this amount; were there no barges there would have to be space for 385 hopper cars or 1,000 trucks to arrive, await their turns, unload, and move away. This apart from the economy of the barge mode.

For some years now the river operators and the railroads have been arguing over such things as BTUs of energy per ton/mile and shipping costs. A layman is at something of a loss to understand the force of their arguments, but the general idea seems to be that both modes are energy-efficient — about two-and-a-half times as efficient per ton/mile as a pipeline, three-and-a-half as much as a truck, and 90 times as much as a plane — and that barge costs per ton/mile are much lower than in any other mode, though the indirect course of the river may require more miles from point to point. In any case, river transportation has grown enormously in the last few decades, especially in the Pittsburgh area. The Port of Pittsburgh, which extends 40 miles down the Ohio to the state line, 30 miles up the Allegheny to include Freeport, and 43 miles up the Monongahela to include Charleroi, is the busiest inland river port in the nation; in a recent year it handled 41 million tons of cargo.

Recently, the river and rail operators have been exploring the idea of "intermodalism," a balanced system of transportation that would allow each mode to do what it can do best: a truce in rivalries going back a century or more, and possibly good business for everyone. □

One of the Port of Pittsburgh's many river terminals, from which goods are shipped and received. This is a private terminal, run by a company for its own goods; but there are also "public" terminals, where anyone can transship the goods they are equipped to handle (below).

THE RIVERS AS A SYSTEM

The often-ragged shoreline of the rivers, overhung with trees and bushes that grow uninhibited, disguises the fact that these rivers are actually part of a system, governed by complex considerations and controlled, upstream and down, by enormous engineering works. We have become dependent on the rivers' being confined to certain levels. Too much water and the valleys are flooded; too little water and vessels ground, water intakes of towns and factories become high and dry, and pollutants that are tolerable when diluted are concentrated in what water there is.

All of the Ohio and Monongahela, and some of the Allegheny are canalized, guaranteeing a minimum of water in their pools barring accident. But the locks and dams that let the vessels through while holding the water back have been a sore point for years with river operators and the Army Engineers. There are two major problems. First, they are made of materials — steel and concrete mainly — and materials deteriorate. Lock chamber walls begin to crack and crumble, valves wear out, and watertight seals begin to leak. Second, a lock is a bottleneck; locking through takes time, and the fewer and faster the lockings the better for everyone. In the early 1970s the trend was toward fewer and higher dams, with locks big enough to take the largest modern tows. Reconstruction on the Ohio had almost reached Pennsylvania when a suit over a Mississippi River dam, brought by environmentalists and railroad companies — the river operators' old rivals — resulted in such interferences with major construction that 48 steps are needed for it now, and one group concerned with the matter claims that 25 years can elapse between the felt need for a new or reconstructed dam and its completion. Even repairs involve red tape. In Pennsylvania, then, large tows on the Ohio lock through in two parts with other tows expensively awaiting their turns.

While the river dams are holding the water back, letting through only enough to maintain pool levels, 15 reservoirs upstream are controlling the water that will come down the Allegheny and the Monongahela. The Pittsburgh Engineer District, an arbitrary-looking blob on the map of the states, actually covers all the water that will come to the Ohio above the District's terminal point at New Martinsville, West Virginia. The reservoirs are intended to control this water near its origins, letting enough get into the rivers but not too much. Success is not absolute; floods still happen. But most of the dams were in place when Tropical Storm Agnes hit in 1972, and without them the flood level at Pittsburgh would have been 12 feet higher, 32 feet above pool level; they would have taken 11 feet off even the flood of 1936, 38 feet above the pool level at that time, had they then existed.

Controlling the dams is done from Pittsburgh, a procedure with complexities and sometimes compromises. The weather of the next few months has to be anticipated so that each reservoir will have neither too much nor too little water when the time comes. Decisions over release of warmer water from the upper part of a dam or cooler water from the lower part have to be made, since river fish have limited temperature tolerances. The reservoirs are used for recreational boating, and this suggests a narrow range of water levels in them. Sometimes extra water is demanded too, to dilute downstream pollution.

Pollution, though, is much less of a problem than it used to be. Private industry has been conforming, though ruefully, to the standards set (and sometimes revised) by Federal and State agencies, and spending heavily in the process. Thermal pollution, hostile to aquatic life and caused by heated water from power plants and steel mills, has been defeated by such things as cooling towers, the diabolo-shaped constructions 500 feet high that signal a modern power plant. Where once a river near a steel mill might get to 130 degrees, it is now almost at natural temperature. Sewage is being treated with more or less success, and Alcosan, which services Pittsburgh and many other local communities, claims that its effluent is purer than the Ohio

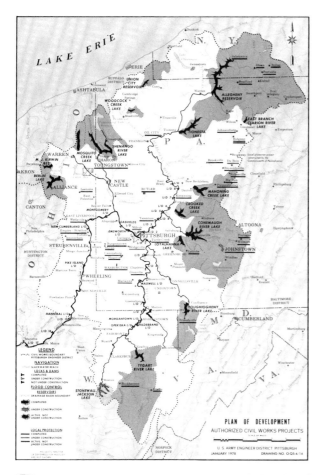

PLAN OF DEVELOPMENT
AUTHORIZED CIVIL WORKS PROJECTS

U.S. ARMY ENGINEER DISTRICT PITTSBURGH
JANUARY 1978   DRAWING NO: O-QS-4-14

The Pittsburgh District of the U.S. Army Corps of Engineers includes the Ohio River above New Martinsville, West Virginia, and all water that flows into it. The Port of Pittsburgh includes the Ohio down to the state line (40 miles), the Monongahela to and including Charleroi (43 miles), and the Allegheny to and including Freeport, just below the Kiskiminetas (30 miles).

An excursion boat enters the smaller "river" chamber of the Emsworth Locks. The chambers seem vast, but the "land" chamber, 600 feet long by 110 feet wide, is half the length needed for modern tows. In Pennsylvania, large tows must lock through on the Ohio in two parts, with a compounding of the expense and delay if several are approaching at the same time.

River water it joins. There is still some pollution from sewage, industrial wastes, and drainage from abandoned mines, but fish are thriving in all parts of the rivers, and are generally edible.

A few worried parties, on the other hand, are looking ahead to occasions when the Monongahela might have a water quantity problem. Water is pulled out of all the rivers in huge amounts, and not all of it is returned. The Ohio, by the time it reaches the state line, has been used twice for industrial, municipal, and various other purposes. The Allegheny at Freeport has been used four times, and the Monongahela, Beaver, Conemaugh, and Kiskiminetas, at their mouths, six or seven times. Industry especially is given to "consumptive use" of water: in other words, the water goes up in steam. It takes 35,000 gallons to get a ton of steel to the semi-finished state, and a good portion of this rises in majestic clouds above the river valleys, eventually to fall to earth. A cooling tower, though it recirculates 95 percent of the water it cools, still evaporates as much as 10,000 gallons a minute. The demands for water, especially on the industrial Monongahela, will increase, and the river could find itself overworked. □

Each of the cooling towers built near the former nuclear power station at Shippingport on the Ohio is 500 feet high, and is capable of cooling 500,000 gallons of condenser water a minute, losing 10,000 gallons to evaporation.

The Kinzua Dam, which impounds the Allegheny Reservoir: 190 billion gallons of water, held or released as conditions on the Allegheny and Ohio rivers indicate.

RECREATION
─ ON THE RIVERS ─

Swimmers at Sistersville, West Virginia, pose for a portrait in 1918.

RECREATION ON THE RIVERS

The cleaner conditions of recent years have encouraged more and more people to see the rivers as recreational places, to walk beside the water or get out upon it. Marinas abound, and small wonder since there are 22,000 motorboats in Allegheny County, almost triple the next-highest figure for Pennsylvania of Bucks County. Water-skiing is popular a few miles up the Allegheny, and canoeing is very popular further up, in the northern part of the state. Slippery Rock Creek, feeding into the Beaver River, is a kayaking stream, and the lower Youghiogheny between Ohiopyle and Connellsville is one of the two whitewater rafting areas in the state. People are discovering all these places and making use of them, attracted by the challenge, and paradoxically the peace, to be found with the rivers.

Aiding the popularity of the rivers for recreation is the Three Rivers Regatta, sponsored by the Port Authority of Allegheny County, the City of Pittsburgh, and many public and private organizations. Started in 1978, the Regatta is intended to advertise the rivers as places for work and enjoyment. Festive river events continue for several days in great variety: marine parades like those of Pittsburgh's past river festivals, races by motor-powered sternwheelers, an "anything that floats" competition and swimming races across the Allegheny, water-skiing demonstrations, sailing, canoeing and kayaking events, balloon ascensions, whistle-blowing, hang-gliding, among other things. The Regattas have a great turnout; the nine-day Regatta of 1981 had 800,000 attendances.

Point State Park during a Three Rivers Regatta.

The Three Rivers Regatta marine parade (above) continues Pittsburgh's tradition of riverboat parades.

Whether fishing, boating or swimming, the rivers of Pittsburgh are a source of recreation for people of all ages and talents.

Simply being beside the water on an ordinary day is a pleasure in itself; yet though there are grand proposals for waterfront parks, places at the water's edge meant for leisure are still few. Kittanning, Tarentum, and Brackenridge on the Allegheny have parks, as do McKeesport on the Monongahela and Beaver on the Ohio, and the Engineer dams sometimes have park-like areas by the water.

But the showplace remains Point State Park at Pittsburgh. This park, completed in 1974, has 36 acres of lawns, shrubs, trees, and waterside landings where boats can tie up. It has an open-air summer stage for the Pittsburgh Symphony Orchestra, and the American Wind Symphony's stage-barge, *Point Counterpoint II*, often is moored at the Allegheny River landing. Point State Park is a natural focus for great public events that take place during the warm months. It also is a reminder of Pittsburgh history. The perimeter of Fort Duquesne is outlined on the ground, and two of the bastions of the vastly more powerful Fort Pitt have been reproduced to house the Fort Pitt Museum. The 1764 block-house, a five-sided redoubt of Fort Pitt, is an authentic remain and the oldest existing building in the Golden Triangle. Finally, the Royal American Regiment, with eighteenth-century costumes and weaponry, stages mock battles at Point State Park during the summer.

The focal point of the Park is the great fountain, which draws its water from the city's "fourth river," the subterranean Wisconsin Flow. The fountain sends up 6,000 gallons a

minute in a 150-foot jet under normal conditions, but sometimes the jet goes as high as 200 feet when the air is still. In fact, it has reached 320 feet without any difficulty.

Of course, the formality of a park is not really necessary. There are wharfs and riverbanks, and many find these good enough for sitting, fishing, and swimming. Until 1950 the tip of the Point was a tree-grown, weedy bit of leftover land beyond the Manchester and Point bridges. Workers came for a lunchtime nap on the grass, flowers grew on the steep banks, and barges tied up at their edges: quite disorganized but decidedly pleasant. All along the rivers, boys especially still make do with the exiguous, overgrown strips of shore that railroads and the highways have left.

The excursion-boat tradition is an old one in Pittsburgh, as in any river town. The view of the features of the land from an unfamiliar place, the gentle motion of the boat itself, the casting-off of ordinary cares that seems to coincide with the throwing-in of the hawser from the wharf, and the thrill that a landsman may feel, for a complexity of half-understood reasons, from the very awareness of being *on a boat* are elements of a pleasure not to be experienced in any other way.

The grand old boats of the past are with us no longer. The Streckfus sidewheeler *Senator* was put out of action in 1941, and the *Delta Queen*, a California river boat but at least a steam stern-wheeler, has ceased to call regularly at Pittsburgh.

The band of Eisenbarth-Henderson Floating Theatre (top), one of the most famous showboats early in this century. "View the Parade" — that is, the marine parade at the 1908 Sesquicentennial (middle). Towboats and packets along the Monongahela Wharf during the Pittsburgh Sesquicentennial celebration of 1908 (bottom).

Those who go out on the water at Pittsburgh today do so on the boats of the Gateway Clipper Fleet. The Fleet has prospered since its beginning in 1958 and maintains a busy schedule, especially in the summer, with a large variety of day and night cruises that range near and far. The two-hour Three Rivers Cruise from the Station Square landing goes up the Monongahela as far as the Jones & Laughlin plant, down the Ohio to McKees Rocks Bridge, and up the Allegheny as far as the H. J. Heinz plant, giving an all-around view of the city: its hills, its neighborhoods, its industries, its skyline, and the great fountain at the Point.

There are many other cruises also, shorter and longer. Of these, some are mainly for sightseeing, and then the boat may be out all day — up the Allegheny to Kittanning, up the Mononga-

hela to Brownsville, or far down the Ohio: for instance, a Fall Foliage Cruise, a Lock and Dam Cruise, a cruise to Old Economy Village where the Harmony Society lived, or a Twilight Fountain Cruise for viewing the Point Park fountain floodlit in gold. Other cruises are more in the nature of parties on the water, usually centered on themes: ethnic nights or dance cruises, each appealing to some special group of passengers and many times offering dinner and live entertainment; the variety of these seems to be infinite. Other cruises are for everyone: the Captain's Dinner Dance Cruise, the Moonlight Dance Cruise, or the Goodship Lollipop Cruise, with Lolli the Clown on board.

John E. Connelly, president of the Gateway Clipper Fleet, conceived the idea in 1956 of reviving riverboat cruises after seeing an excur-

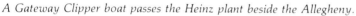

A Gateway Clipper boat passes the Heinz plant beside the Allegheny.

sion-boat operation in Chicago. The rivers of Pittsburgh were the obvious vantage points for seeing the city at that time, when its nationally-famous Renaissance I had already built new office towers and cleaned the air. Pittsburghers had enjoyed boat excursions in the past, and after two decades without much opportunity for them, they took gladly to Connelly's first small boat, the *Gateway Clipper,* and to the larger and larger boats that followed. So did out-of-towners, here to see the Renaissance city. Today a boat excursion is one of the things a visitor does, and charter buses arrive from as far as Canada for the purpose of going on a cruise.

The Gateway Clipper Fleet's operation today is the largest of its kind in the United States, with vessels ranging from a small 150-passenger riverboat to one that carries 1,000 passengers. Many of the dinner-dance cruises go out on the *Gateway Party Liner,* a floating ballroom with an ample floor, which holds 600 on a daytime tour and 400 on a dance cruise. Many Pittsburgh organizations use it, too, for meetings and banquets afloat. The boats are used not only for cruises; the Fleet operates a shuttle service, taking passengers from Station Square or the Monongahela Wharf to Three Rivers Stadium, Point State Park, and the David L. Lawrence Convention Center.

In 1982 the Gateway Clipper Fleet moved to Station Square, opposite their base of 24 years at the Monongahela Wharf. Station Square, a continuing adaptive-use project of Pittsburgh History & Landmarks Foundation, is the largest of its kind in the nation. Landmarks has adapted the historic terminal buildings and warehouses of the Pittsburgh & Lake Erie Railroad for commercial, business, and cultural use, and the 41-acre area has become one of the busiest places in town, virtually a new city within a city where pleasure is as important as work. The move to Station Square for the Clipper Fleet cost $4,000,000, but shoppers can now go on a short cruise, tourists can visit a multitude of luxury shops, and everyone, buyer and seller, stands to gain. □

The Pittsburgh & Lake Erie Railroad buildings and yards, the headquarters of a "little giant" among railroads that is still thriving on freight traffic, are now being developed as Station Square. When begun in 1976, Station Square was the largest adaptive-use project in the nation, and the first major commercial development in downtown Pittsburgh to take advantage of its riverfront location. The Gateway Clipper Fleet now docks at Station Square, and millions of Pittsburghers and tourists come to visit each year.

A Gateway Clipper boat passes the Three Rivers Stadium, the home of the Pirates and Steelers.

A crew of cousins aboard the Goodship Lollipop.

THE RIVERS AND PITTSBURGH

For two centuries and a half the rivers of the Pittsburgh area have served two kingdoms, a republic, and a multitude of industrialists and merchants pursuing their ambitions. Towns have deposited their filth into the rivers, and towns also have drunk from them. They have been *used,* in short, for material purposes both good and bad. Smoke has risen in billows from their shores, and the surface of the water has been covered with deep-laden barges of coal, awaiting the chance to move away. Yet even at their most satanically industrial time there remained something alluring about the tarnished silver surfaces that wound between the hills and plains: that abrupt halt to the land, and a river flowing turbulently or placidly, much as it had for thousands of years, toward a far-off sea.

Pittsburgh's beauty is in its spaces: in the many chances there are, in and around the city, to look down, or up, or away, and see clustered houses, shrubs, and trees, hills like tossing waves, fretted skylines of roofs and chimneys, ridges beyond ridges under a variegated light as the clouds pass over. No great matter if you are — and you probably are — standing at the edge of a dreary street, looking, if you only knew, toward a multitude of other dreary streets: the distances are great enough, and the contours of the land are overmastering enough, that you are encouraged to imagine that over *there* it is all beautiful.

And the rivers, which long ago carved the hills, give vitality to the whole scene as the most overmastering element of all. They appear in different colors, and odd textures cover parts of their surfaces, apparently without cause. Sometimes they are slick as wax, sometimes minutely ruffled like a silver-gray felt, sometimes blown into little waves, sometimes marbled with ice. The surface quality of the land changes slowly with the seasons for the most part, but the surface of a river, seen from a hillside, is different from one day to the next. □

Picture Credits

John L. Alexandrowicz: p. 8(bottom), p. 9, p. 71.

Carnegie Library of Pittsburgh: p. 10, p. 11(top left & bottom), p. 13(bottom), p. 14, p. 19, p. 24, p. 25(top), p. 34, p. 35, p. 46.

Drake Well Museum: p. 7(top).

Dravo Corporation: p. 42, p. 43, p. 49(top right & bottom), p. 50, p. 51, p. 52, p. 53(top right), p. 56, p. 57(bottom).

Duquesne Light Company: p. 60(top).

Gateway Clipper Fleet: p. iv, p. 16(top), p. 59(bottom), p. 64(top left), p. 65(bottom), p. 67, p. 68(top), p. 69(top left), p. 72(middle right).

Clyde Hare: Front, back and inside covers, p. i, p. 3, p. 4, p. 5, p. 7(bottom), p. 15(bottom), p. 37(top), p. 44, p. 45(top), p. 47(bottom), p. 48, p. 49(top left), p. 53(top left & bottom), p. 63(top right, bottom left & right), p. 64(top right, bottom left & right), p. 69(bottom), p. 70, p. 72(left, top & bottom right), p. 73.

The Historical Society of Western Pennsylvania: p. 11(top right), p. 15(top).

Library of Congress Mississippi River Views collection; from the steamboat photo collection of G. W. "Jerry" Sutphin: p. 17(bottom).

Pittsburgh History & Landmarks Foundation: p. 8(top), p. 26(top right, bottom left & right—gift of Mrs. W. E. Fels), p. 31(gift of the Richard King Mellon Foundation), p. 37(bottom—gift of Mrs. W. E. Fels), p. 38, p. 63(top left), p. 75.

Pittsburgh & Lake Erie Railroad: p. 66(bottom).

Pittsburgh 3 Rivers Regatta: p. 62, p. 63(middle right).

John Shryock: p. 36(bottom), p. 45(bottom), p. 54, p. 65(top).

G. W. "Jerry" Sutphin: p. 23.

Mrs. John R. Thorne: p. 69(top right).

U.S. Army Corps of Engineers: p. 13(top right), p. 16(bottom), p. 21(from Frederick B. Read, *Up the Heights of Fame and Fortune,* 1873), p. 22(top—from Frederick B. Read, *Up the Heights of Fame and Fortune,* 1873), p. 39(bottom), p. 55(from *Monongahela River Navigation Charts,* January 1979), p. 59(top), p. 60(bottom).

United States Steel Corporation: p. 57(top).

Captain Frederick Way, Jr.: p. iii, p. 17(top), p. 18(bottom), p. 20, p. 27, p. 28, p. 29, p. 32, p. 33, p. 36(top), p. 39(top), p. 41, p. 47(top), p. 61, p. 66(top & middle right).

Western Pennsylvania Conservancy: p. 2(bottom left), p. 6, p. 18(top).

Illustrations: p. 22(bottom—from *A Textbook on Marine Engineering,* Scranton, Pa., International Textbook Company, 1900), p. 25(bottom—from Archer Butler Hulbert's *Historic Highways of America*), p. 26(top left—from *James Rees & Sons Company, Illustrated Catalog,* 1913).

Reading about the Rivers

The S&D Reflector, the illustrated quarterly of the Sons and Daughters of Pioneer Rivermen, is a fine source of river history from the steamboat period. Despite the society's name, pedigree is not important in joining. For membership information, write to Mrs. J. W. Rutter, 964 Worthington, Birmingham, Michigan 48009.

Steamboat Bill, the illustrated quarterly of the Steamship Historical Society of America, is concerned with shipping worldwide but gives current Western River news regularly. If you would like to join, write to Steamship Historical Society of America, 345 Blackstone Boulevard, H. C. Hall Building, Providence, Rhode Island 02906.

The *Port of Pittsburgh Fact Finder* gives essential information on the Port and outlying areas for commercial users and recreationists. Call the Port Authority of Allegheny County at (412) 237-7470.

The Headwaters District is basically a history of the Pittsburgh District of the Army Engineers, but is full of river history generally and is very well illustrated. *Ohio River Navigation: Past—Present—Future* is a small but good book of the same sort, and is free. Both can be obtained from Office of Administrative Services, U.S. Army Corps of Engineers, 1000 Liberty Avenue, Pittsburgh, Pennsylvania 15222. The Public Affairs Officer of the Pittsburgh District also has free pamphlets on the river dams and the upstream reservoirs.

The pool towboat Enterprise, *1898.*

Acknowledgments

To Captain Frederick Way, Jr., for comments on the historic text and for many of the photographs used as illustrations;

Richard Nissley of Mon River Towing, Inc., for comments on the chapters regarding modern navigation;

Cornelis van Mook of Dravo Corporation, for his account of a modern towboat;

Trish Allison of Dravo Corporation, for finding a number of our illustrations;

G. W. ("Jerry") Sutphin of the Huntington District, U.S. Army Corps of Engineers, for lending us illustration material;

John Reed, public affairs officer, and other members of the Pittsburgh District, U.S. Army Corps of Engineers, for supplying literature, illustrations, and answers to questions;

John Connelly and the Gateway Clipper Fleet, for numerous illustrations and information;

Letitia C. Langord and Randy Strothman, for a trip to Marietta and for showing footage of their film *Working River;*

Vincent A. Nese, for granting permission to take the photograph of Station Square from the roof of the House Building, Four Smithfield Street;

the Western Pennsylvania Conservancy, for illustrations and information;

The Historical Society of Western Pennsylvania, for supplying illustrations; and

Carnegie Library of Pittsburgh, for assistance in research and in providing illustrations.

The Three Rivers was typeset in Paladium by Cold-Comp, and was printed on Velvetlith Matte text by Herbick & Held Printing Company. Edited by Louise King Ferguson and designed by Thomas S. Stevenson, Jr., with the assistance of Jacqueline Snyder, of Pittsburgh History & Landmarks Foundation.